Voice from the Soul of Trees

*a collection of inspirational poetry
and prose on life and hope*

CELESTINE MCMULLEN ALLEN

iUniverse, Inc.
New York   Bloomington

Voice from the Soul of Trees
a collection of inspirational poetry and prose on life and hope

iUniverse books may be ordered through booksellers or by contacting:

iUniverse
1663 Liberty Drive
Bloomington, IN 47403
www.iuniverse.com
1-800-Authors (1-800-288-4677)

Because of the dynamic nature of the Internet, any Web addresses or links contained in this
book may have changed since publication and may no longer be valid. The views expressed
in this work are solely those of the author and do not necessarily reflect the views of the
publisher, and the publisher hereby disclaims any responsibility for them.

ISBN: 978-1-4502-3767-3 (pbk)
ISBN: 978-1-4502-3768-0 (ebk)

Printed in the United States of America

iUniverse rev. date: 8/17/10

Dedications

"The soul of the tree lies in the strength of its limbs and roots."

Celestine McMullen Allen

This book is first and foremost, dedicated to my parents, William and Helen McMullen. They genetically gave me my heart and my spirit. Even though they are both deceased, they continually live in my *soul*. They gave me the strength and fortitude to never give up on life. They gave me an understanding of our beautiful and complex world and how our life experiences shape our foundation and build our character. They instilled in me the value of embracing life, learning from it, and living through it. Even as a child, I knew that a broad array of experiences were before me. Even as a child, I felt like I was an old soul. I was always like the fly on the wall; listening and learning from my elders. I did not understand the extent of what I was hearing then; yet, I always had that sense of "knowing" that "life "would find me; and it did.

My parents' love and the lessons they instilled in me have transcended time. They etched their markings upon me; and as in my birth and rebirth, they gave me the seed that long ago, was deemed to sprout in the manner my life unfolded. The seeds they planted included an understanding of mankind, human nature, and valuing people who cross your path. These lessons are their legacy of life and hope for me and my siblings from *"under the pecan tree"*.

I also dedicate this book to my nephew, Danis Ennis McMullen. Whether we realized it, sooner or later, our spirits ran in parallel. Unfortunately, Danis' life ended July 26, 2009. He lived through his own personal travails. Yet, *"when he wanted to claim the world, it was his. It was our pleasure to stand back and watch."* His attitude towards life epitomized hope. He created his own legacy; his own strong branch. He, too, lived *"under the pecan tree"*.

This book is also dedicated to my grandparents, uncles, aunts, and cousins that are no longer with us; Laura and James McMullen, Leila and Ivory Barnes, Aunt Marie, Uncle James, Aunt Verna, Uncle Jesse, Aunt Ethel, Uncle Albert, Uncle Doc, Uncle Lint, Uncle Charlie, Aunt Gladys, Uncle Ike, Aunt Lillian, Bay Brother, Mildred and Frank. Your love impacted my world and kept me grounded in the roots of my tree.

Acknowledgements

"The soul of the tree lies in the bounty of the fruit it bears".

Celestine McMullen Allen

My acknowledgements include loved ones, both living and deceased, who also impacted my life, instilled hope, and who continue to grace me with their love and life lessons. There are so many people that have had positive influences on me. I am remiss for not mentioning everyone by name or inadvertently missing a limb on my tree. It is not because of lack of love for you nor from knowing how important you are to me.

In keeping with the theme of the book, the people in my life are like a grove or a forest of beautiful trees; sharing love, co-existing together. I see your beauty in sturdy dogwoods that can live in the wilderness and bare beautiful flowers; as groves of pecan trees that provide shade and hearty crops of their own fruit; cherry trees; delicate, seasonal, and with blossoms that blow away with the wind, returning in their own season; weeping willows with their draping limbs singing their own graceful song and providing a sweet protective covering; strong, tall pine trees with deep roots that show their strength in their heartiness; pine saplings that stand as little soldiers until they are ready to serve their purpose in life; or mighty oak trees with branches broad enough to provide love for the world. I have sat under these trees and have been graced with their bounty.

I have to start from the branches of my pecan tree; my brothers and sisters and their children, now bringing forth more branches. I am the youngest of seven siblings. To my brothers and sisters, William, Brenda, Ralph, Roland, Calvin, and Rita, thanks for being wonderful role models. We shared life together. We laughed together. We cried together. I remember the times that I had to "fight" to be more than a "baby" sister in your lives. After years of ironing your shirts, oiling your scalps, hanging out with you, being the instant and willing babysitter, maturing together; regardless of the ranges in our ages, my triumphs came. We have a bond that is predicated upon knowing that we are one in the spirit of our parents.

My life was enriched from the bonds my siblings forged; Gwendolyn, Jim, Amelia, Rebecca, Martha, and Lowe. You saw me grow up. You gave me love, thus, enhancing my experiences in life. And you gave me beautiful and strong nieces and nephews. I began my auntie duties at the ripe age of nine. And now, my nieces and nephews are sprouting their own limbs on "our" tree. This makes me a Great Auntie. The children; their seed, are the ones who will keep our legacy strong.

Gregory, my husband, you made the ultimate sacrifice. Understanding the legacy and in understanding me, we have grown our own limb on the tree. You allowed me the opportunity to find my way, harness my strength; and to understand how I was to impact the world. You knew that I could never be my "true self" until I sprouted. I love you, and my family loves you like a brother. You, too, are a strong role model for all of our babies. And with our union, another branch emerged; Momma Ella, Dexter, Wyattnetta, and Darryl. Our union represents another strong branch on the tree. The seed of their seed are our babies too.

I have to include my cousins in this acknowledgement; the seed and branches of our parent's seed, our grandparents. For part of the journey, we grew up together, lived in different geographical areas, or went on divergent paths; and cultivated other trees; still a part of my forest. Collectively, we have always had special relationships. We have always known that our love for one another is as strong as our *deep roots and hovering branches.*

There are others; I call them my extended families. The Byrd family, who treated me like a daughter, a grand-daughter, a sister, and a friend. They were there when I lost everything to an apartment fire. The Williams family; never a hiccup in love shared, our bond, nor my place in their lives; bringing forth more and more love from all types of trees. The Barnes family; (Bessie, her mother, and her sisters) represented sisterhood and camaraderie - forever a bond. The Griffins – George and Venice and their families; my sister and brother forming more branches of fortifying strength and love. These branches also include Jack Hyatt; his family, Ginger and George Mayer; Pat Hall Jaynes and her family; Phil Mitchell; his family, Clarence Kornegay, and Oretha Harper; Cindy McKinnon; her family; Sam and Joyce Perryman, their families; and Locy Baker and his family. We have all forged bonds of a lifetime. The definitions of relationships with my extended families still continue to grow as strong branches on my tree.

Special thanks to Venice for her ear throughout this project and to Mitt Kirkland, Mamie Williams, and Oretha Harper for lending their voice and poetic souls to finalize this collection.

"Praise to God for the life that I have lived and the people who are a limb of my tree. For with these souls, my life has been enhanced."

Celestine McMullen Allen

Introduction

Voice from the Soul of Trees

Even before you read the first poem in this collection, I would like to set the stage for what the book is about. The book provides a contrast of nature and life, their parallel collage; their montage; and a voice that blends them together. Life, as we all experience it, does not have a singular dimension. Neither does this collection of poetry. But what it does provide is a focus on our collective entities; you, I, and mankind embracing, and living life as one; beyond boundaries. First, we are one with self; and secondarily, we are one with the world in which we live together; especially our loved ones.

The resonant analogy is with nature, man, and living. The dominate figure in this collection is the tree; nature; and how nature and life work together. Trees have always intrigued me. They represent how life can comingle, and how they can create their own palette just as sisters and brothers, uncles and aunts, nieces and nephews, cousins, extended family members, friends, co-workers, acquaintances; people that challenge you; people that protect you, and people that love you; a universal tree.

My initial inspiration came from this strong pecan tree that was in the backyard of my homestead. The tree was strong, stout, and sturdy; *"hovering limbs, knotty branches, and deep roots"*. This tree represented life on so many levels. It was more than a tree that provided "spending money" in her season of bounty or a tree that represented the "toil" of having to rack her abundant leaves. This tree represented wisdom; life; living; being grounded; strength of mankind, shelter, and unity.

So with this frame of reference, I look to all trees to provide the same lessons. I can ride along the countryside, and see a tree, and become inspired by its' beauty. I can feel the life that emits from her roots; her branches; her strength and her spirit. I see trees co-mingling together; oftentimes a unique family relying on the natural order of life to dictate their unique place.

Reminiscent of life, our distinctive styles of living, and our sometimes disjointed realities, I look to the soul of the tree. It is from this perspective that I have penned this collection of poetry and prose. The uniqueness of the tree; in varying seasons, bless us with their flowers or their fruit. In varying seasons, the fruit is bountiful. In varying seasons, they lay dormant; bearing the harshness of cold winters. In varying seasons, we only see the stumps of their existence. In the spring of their season, they give us new trees strong enough to bear *"strong branches, knotty limbs, and deep roots."*

Celestine McMullen Allen

Chapter I

-

On Life

The Tree of my Voice

Let the virtues of man
Shine through the tree like a sunrise
Let the wisdom of life
Flow through me like a sunset
Let the moon cast her light
Infiltrating, illuminating, and beaming bright
Seek shelter in the branches of the tree
Let her barrenness speak of hope
Let the sprigs of new life, her fruit, and blossoms
Speak of new life
Let the bounty of the seasons
Bear fruit worthy of the harvest
Let the glory of the splendor of her colors
Shine full reign in her seasons
Let the age of her message
Speak to man
Her glory reigns beyond principalities
Beyond regions, continental divides
Oceans and beliefs
For a tree, planted in due season
Shall bloom and bear much fruit
Seeds, spewing forth
Yield nations of men united
The harvest, the beauty
Feeding souls in Thanksgiving bounty
Rising sap of the saplings
Soldiers for the harvest to come
Delicate dancers of her flowering kin
Bond together to provide shelter from the storm
Give me my tree of peace
Give me my tree of shelter
Give me my tree of grace
Give me the tree of my voice

The Palm

Within the palm of my hand, I hold a mighty tool
Capable of capturing, molding, and disseminating the mysteries of life
With a pen in hand
I reflect on love, sadness, victory, and strife
I share the voice of my soul
That which has molded me and which has made me cry, sigh, and shout with glee
Folded up, fist clenched
I depict strength of will and inner fortitude
I share the manifestation of my spirit
My convictions gleaned from holding strong, holding on, and knowing when to bow
Gently curved
I bestow the softest touch
I share the subtleties of my femininity; the outpouring of my soul in its' trinity
Combining all parts of me which make me whole
Giving and receiving love
In any manifestation
There is a desire to possess only that which is real
There is no fear of loss
Only that which I need to depart from
There is no grasping
Reaching out
To that which is mine

Dancing To the Tunes of Life

My life is a word
Poetic melodies, that when combined, reflect who I am
Why I cry, why I am remise, and why sometimes
I am so elated that I dance with the sun
My life is a song
Melodic tunes that peal truths, calling me by my name
Songs that pierce my existence
Bearing the vulnerabilities of my soul
The words, they are my vehicle; my journey to unfold
The song gives flight to my dreams
The interwoven tunes of life play before me
I connect with me
As I listen to the melodies
I become closer to my being
My evolution of living
Its essence, its sights, and its sounds
On one journey, I am a dancer
Living life as I express the heartbeat of my soul
The melodies manifest in the movement of my feet
Higher and higher I reach out to the songs that pulsate within me
My body sways to the tunes
My heart blends with the rhythms
My soul lives the notes
On another journey, I become a musician
I'm one with the bongo
As it beats the basic foundation of my existence
My strength and my endurance
Helping me to understanding life
Me, and the person that I am in my most primal state
I'm one with the piano, providing contrast and balance
Either playing an overture exalting in my triumphs and victories
Or playing an upbeat staccato as I prance through life
Knowing where I am going
I'm one with the saxophone, wailing the blues of my existence
Releasing any hurt or pain

Allowing only true expressions of love
My songs peal of ballads
Their earthiness depicting serenity and true communion
And how my world unfolds
My songs peal of the gospel
Peace be still, temper me, balance me, focus me
Help me to keep my eye on the sparrow
As the notes and song are orchestrated
Poetically or musically
I dance to the tunes and stanzas of life
Embracing their messages
I flow with the beat of any composition
I live and understand life.

Retrospection

There are places that we all go in our head
Traveling deep within the recesses of our soul
Long journeys
That lead to places
That sometimes, we would rather forget
While on this journey
We can either block out
We can strike out
Or we embrace
Then we heal.

Reality and Heart Decisions

Heart decisions create a reality
Founded in the strength of grains of sand
We seek love
The goal to be happy
To fill an internal void or find our soul
We have a plan
Our goal spurred on by past hurts
Our plan based on misplaced values
Fronting
As real as the reality
Circumstances
Create our actions
We sometimes misread relationships that enter into our path
Decision time
Survival instincts kick in
Creating opportunities for false realities of the heart
We pay for the lack of loving self
The reality is
That we all seek love
And when love is lost, we settle
We wallow in an existence of holding back emotionally
Not making good decisions for self
We create internal wars and external effects
Mirroring role models of how life should not be
The reality is
We all have choices of the heart
A choice to build our personal foundation
A choice to not partake
In situations that create personal turmoil
Should I, or could I have
The reality is
Decisions affect our personal lives and those around us
Decisions drive our actions, good, bad, or indifferent
The reality is
True love for self conquers all
The reality is
Negative actions creep in to feel the voids.

Revelations

Not an end, but a beginning
Life isn't idealized, it is lived
An on-going quest for peace, tranquility, and balance
With the capacity to love as the means
The search for self love first
But when we find that place
We live a life of Godliness
Our actions are of God
Our efforts are of God
The bounty of our fruit is of God.

Creation, Procreation, and My Existence

Lying in the afterbirth, cauls still intact
I lay atop my mother's womb
One day, two days, three days
My existence defined by hearing first, then seeing
From this stalled emergence into this world
My childhood, my youth, and my adulthood
My ongoing creation still defining the me that I am
A child, treading paths
A child, rebelling against being forced to a fit into a mold
I claim this person that I was born to be in
My creation, my procreation, and my existence
As a young adult, I let me define my way
No to conformity
Yes, to self-acceptance
Yes to yearning and finding my way
No to succumbing
Still claiming this person that I was born to be
My creation, my procreation, and my existence
The unknowns, that which was to be
Living a path of future dreams
Growing, living and learning
The balancing act
The me of my mother and my father
Recognizing the blessing of this understanding
Of wise counsel, humility, and strength
Treading their paths
Living the path of what was to transpire
Growing, listening, living, and learning
Being me, fully enmeshed, embracing all, still defining my person
A young adult, on a different and sometimes ill-defined path
Still focused, still triumphant over life's trials
Continuing to grow, continuing to understand me
Overcoming; persevering
Knowing the cause
I claim this person

A woman now
Even new levels of adversity brings
New levels of peace, new levels of strength
Calling upon God, nature, family and friends
Continually adding to the layers of
My creation, my procreation, and my existence
Re-defined sense of self
Re-defined sense of understanding
Of this place in which I have arrived
An understanding of the important things in life
Being vulnerable
Not afraid to share my story
Being discerning, listening and hearing
Constantly reflecting on life
Staying true to me
Overcoming, and not being overcome
I claim this person that I have matured into
I claim this emergence of hearing first
My creation, my procreation, and my existence
Discernment; constantly reflecting on the big picture
Overcoming and not being overcome

I claim this person that has emerged

Emergence from the Womb

We come out of the womb
Expecting perfect peace
Peace of the womb
A peace that brings serenity
Protected, coddled, and nurtured
Then our unfounded world appears as an illusion
Pacifiers drop from our lips
Hugs we craved but didn't get
Hunger for food that is not fed
Utterance of words not heard
Unmet needs during our formative years
Sometimes, the shield is opaque and fragile
Our outcries may not be heard
We can't burst the bubble
We toddle and eventually gain some independence
We walk, and the layers of unmet needs weigh us down
We cry, but only wipe away surface tears
We feed ourselves, but the internal hunger never ceases
We have yearnings, but as we grow, the needs become stronger
Until we realize the reason for the void;
The meshing of our personal need for love.

I Can't Imagine

I can't imagine not being me
Battered armor
Dents and dings of a warrior
Formed by years of war with a strong adversary
Life
Forging a foundation
Resistant to failure
The armor still shining bright
Shining with the light
The desire to lead a full life
I can't imagine not experiencing my reality
Forged with a zest for living
Able to stand firm against the gusts of displeasure
Bowing gently with the breezes of love
Which blow through my hair
As if to say fly with me
As I can't imagine not being me
I can't imagine my life without the love of God
Always being there as my shield.

Time Changes

Time changes, people adapt
Lives change, and people adjust
Love is lost, and people sell their souls
The strength of love is all powerful
It rules the head with a fiery force
Causing all inhibitions to cease
All restraints to flow free
All options open

Strength in Nurturing

What keeps us from taking that first step?

How does a child know when he is ready to walk?
How does a heart know when it is ready to love?
How does a soul know when it is ready to live?

Strength in nurturing

Is there a threshold?
Is there a common foundation?
Is there a safe haven?
Is there a sense of peace?

Strength in nurturing

Of the first step, it's about nurturing
Of the foundation, it's about nurturing
Of the peace, it's about nurturing

Strength in nurturing

Strength in being and finding our place

It's the nurturing

The Precipice

Imagine being on a mountain
Looking out over the horizon
The ranges speaks of eternal life
For they have been there through the ages of time.
Imagine being on the precipice
Experiencing life
Starting the climb from the bottom
In awe of the landings
Ecstatic from eventually reaching the peak
Looking out at the world for possibilities
Seeing another outlook
From the precipice of life

Spiritual Calm after the Storm

In the rages and the storms
Find solace, for there will be peace
Stand firm against the turbulence
The rain will subside
And the rays of sunshine shall beam down
On this spiritual journey
Walk in this path of the light
Exultation makes a triumphant entrance
Enveloping our dimness in the brightness of light
Like an epiphany, our soul is awakened
The spirit is rekindled
The eyes are open to the love of God
We understand from whence comes our peace
We understand the storm of our existence

Pretentious

Pretend is the game we play
When we want to hide within ourselves
The games are fantasy
A world not visible to all
Play like, fooling the self
Actions of life are like playing tag
We envision the world as a tea cup
Porcelain dolls and rugby brutes
Seeing self as the sole victor
Serving life on a silver platter
Or living life as a challenge on the playing field
No conception or appreciation
For the delicacy or the finesse of the game
No conception of the forces
In the game called real life

Our Journey

I like you, walk a path in this life
Sometimes our paths cross
At times, they run parallel
The destination
Our unique fate
That unfolds with each breath and decision we make
Common to our journeys are
The agonies and the pain
The sunshine and the rain
The smiles and the tears
The lessons we learn
And even our fears
At times, we hold the world in our hands
And claim it as our own
At times, we want to go to the most desolate corner of the earth
To escape a plight that unfolds
And yet, we know we must take this journey
For it leads to our destiny
The journey that makes you, you
And me, me

The Dawning of the Day

My dawning, a renaissance
A rebirth with each newly infused light
No time to go back, for the past is gone
No time to dwell on what was
For it is nevermore
A new way of relating emerges
A new outlook, a new feeling
One to behold and covet
One that cannot be contained
In a cage of wondering and doubt
The new reality says yes
This is how it can be
Only if we bear the dawns
That have come before us
With acceptance of their power
They bring an understanding
That this is how life should be
In this dawning
We're presented with a new day
To feel, to be
And return all of the positive energy
To the universe
That rises within us on each dawning

Flowing Tears, Full Heart

It rained on me last night
The emotions came as a wave, engulfing me
Bringing forth the need to overcome,
Move forward, go beyond
As the tears crested
I braced the storm
To let the tears flow like a mighty river
I braced, the emotions held steadfast
I held on, the emotions subsided
Relenting, letting the flood flow
Releasing as a rhythmic song
Bringing peace to a flowing heart

The Seventh Seed

Nine months in my mothers' womb
Sharing a special bond
Nine months to eternity, she knew the essence of her seed
We lay together on the birthing table
An infinite spirit there for me all of my borne days
Protecting me during our extended stay
Feeding me the afterbirth
My lessons of life
As much as my young soul could consume
Feeding me discernment
Strengthening me
Heightening my perseverance
Fortifying my convictions
Adding layers of empathy for living
Through the eyes of a child
Seeing my place in the beautiful scheme of life
Upon birth, I was nurtured
Upon birth, I was willed strength
Upon birth, my foundation was fortified
Upon living, understanding that I will experience pains
If there be digression, knowing that I will never lose favor
Pursuing unknown paths
Knowing that I will always be led closer to you
At near death, you said, oh no
I've got plans for you
Expecting perfection, you said to me
We all have our flaws
But, I shall give you a beautiful heart
This shall be your way
I shall give you peace
This shall be the seed you will sow
I give you ongoing nourishment
You will keep my roots intact
I will give you discernment
You will know the time

Listen and be patient for your message
Not with a perfect ear
But with a perfect heart
For the feeding made me strong
The feeding made me a hearty seventh seed
My branch, as strong as the six others of our tree

Sincere...Sincerity

In your presence, I get this overwhelming feeling of realness
The kind that defies definition
It takes me to when I was in my mother's womb
The kind, that upon conception, I was nurtured, treasured, and protected
The kind that radiates upon a success, glows in intimacy,
And shudders in a loving embrace—your embrace
In your presence, I am the woman
Sitting high upon a throne
Men grasping at my feet
Women wanting to take my place
You, wanting to be with me
In your presence, I am me
All that I want to be, I am
Any mountain that I encounter, I can climb
My stride gives a clue to my person
My eyes letting the world know
That I have a secret that I don't want to hide
Sincere
As real as real can be
As loving as you'll let me be
Sincere
As we are together

Life Chapters

Wonderful, fruitful chapters
Been given chances
Blind to the opportunities they represented
Been through stuff
Had the nerve to question why me
Been granted opportunities to overcome
Capitalized on some
Lost out on others
But still strong
I can wake up in the early morning
Find peace in my constant dialogue with me
I commune with the dawn
I understand the constant
Each new day brings new levels of understanding
Embracing the rising of the sun
Relishing the hues
Feeling the throbbing pulse of mankind
Feeling centered
Feeling in touch
Feeling love from the universe
Feeling peace
Letting the blessings of the universe guide me
Understanding that life is bigger than me
Bringing me closer to my life
Understand karma
For prior chapters have taught me these lessons
New chapters always unfolding
On a solid foundation for living
A universal grounded life in God's love

Chapter II

-

On Hope

Under the Pecan Tree

Life, like the fruit of the pecan tree has a season
Life, like the seasons of our lives, begins with being nurtured in a
protective shell
The heartiness of our bounty is dependent upon the life giving forces
of our roots
One day, we start falling from the tree
Awaiting our budding, we lay in fertile soil
From our shell, we eventually emerge
Unscathed by the ails of the world
Our fate unknown at the time
Once on the ground, we have to become survivors
Sometimes, oblivious to the wisdom of those overhanging limbs that
protect us
Our shells finally off
We become vulnerable
People gather around to devour our fruit
They pick us and eat of our being like birds of prey
Not understanding that the wisdom of the mighty branches become
a part of them
Even our partakers become again, sheltered like a fresh fallen nut
They find peace
They find comfort
They feel the safe haven from the storm
They feel refreshed
All from partaking of our fruit
For those not picked, we still lay naked
Listening, open and vulnerable, awaiting our fate
Awaiting the wisdom of the pecan tree
We still lay in fertile soil
Our nutrients are replenished
Our ears glued to the ground
We hear the echoing of triumphant tales
Of the knotty limbs, hovering branches, and deep roots
We hear stories of clawing, crawling, clamoring, and overcoming
We regain our strength

We hear stories of life's twists and turns
We re-build our character
We hear stories of overcoming mountains and barriers
We regain our stance
As we listen closer, we understand the lessons
That, even from on high, we can fall down
That from the pits, we can rise up
And that sometimes, if we don't absorb its wisdom
That we just don't do anything but lay there
Play it safe, and stay in the sanctity of our shell, withering away
Those that have come to the pecan tree know that it's not about falling
It's about the fallen fruit that, once bared, is picked up, is cracked open, and savored
Its wisdom crying out to us
Telling us to overcome the seasons of nature and of living
Telling us to survive
Telling us to humbly be
And telling us to have a pure heart
For savoring the fruit of life shall be sweet
Embrace life under the pecan tree
Embrace the plump, succulent fruit of the life lessons
For when seasons pass
They will become barren
Always awaiting a new spring
And another opportunity to bear new fruit

Lunar Messages

I lay, eyes to the darkened sky
And on this night, I see the glory of the presence
Of a luminous quarter moon
Piercing through the sheer of my window
Her palette draped in an aura of darkness
Her hint of light speaking
To the future of brightness in the glimpses of our darkest moment
Shining in her glory, I wonder as to a star
What was I feeling during quarter moons before?
What about the harvest moons before me?
What about the full moon cycles which are to come?
Was I still strong, will I be stronger?
Was I hurting, will the pain ever subside?
Was I experiencing another parallel cycle of life?
And what propels me again
To always look to her future cycles?
With a watchful eye, I see her poignancy
Her splendor, her control
Saying to me that even in this phase
Her cycles dictate more than what is perceived
Her gravitational pulls of existence
Of love and of living
Are not minimized by the mere presence of this quarter moon stage
There is strength in her timing
As a quarter moon
She offers just a little peek
Not wanting to reveal other than glimpses
Of unforeseen, necessary, and unnecessary circumstances of life
Akin to the rain, she feeds and nourishes
And blankets us even in the stillness of the night
Letting us know that she can also bring drought and torrents
As so, can control the emotions of our experiences
Her cycles evolve
She strengthens her presence during the night
As time evolves, she sprinkles moon dust to grace our being

She tests us to see if we are listening
As she emerges in full splendor
A full moon or a harvest moon is presented
Integrating the experiences of prior cycles
She speaks again, asking
Are you strong enough to handle the light that I bring to you in this cycle?
Akin to the sun, she promotes positive life energy
For even against her dark palette
She can determine fruitfulness and seasons of bounty
Akin to our belief and faith in God
She confirms that there is something bigger than us in control
In direct union with God, she can direct the ebb and flow of nature
In direct union with God, she has a hand in the conception of life
In direct union with God, she helps to reward us in bounty
The lunar
That protects us at night
A legacy in the tales of old
Another guide to the timing of our individual life cycles
A marvel of nature
She guides our paths in our darkest moments
Bigger than we will ever know
Her strength available if we choose
To understand the messages of timing in her lunar cycles

Perfect Peace

Peace
    Inner Peace
    Societal Peace
    World Peace
Perfect Peace
One before two
The finding of that inner sanctum
Tiered rewards
 Nurturing of self first
 Private worlds of humility
The beauty of understanding self
The sharing of glimpses of our pure nature
Peace
    Inner Peace
    Societal Peace
    World Peace
Perfect Peace
The wonders of nature marvel us
The sweet song of the birds
The aroma of the flowers
The rising of the moon in its full glory
Praising the loftiness of the clouds
Flowing with the bodies of water
In their tranquil and raging domains
Allowing the rain to fall to quench our souls
Peace
    Inner Peace
    Societal Peace
    World Peace
Perfect Peace
Babes are born
Souls are shaped
Legacies dependent on our openness
To feel, gravitate, rotate, flex, rebound, and be

Distorted Peace
    Personal Greed
    Societal Greed
    World Greed
Imperfect Peace
Fixation on our own agendas
Mystifying, justifying, and quantifying
That which makes us whole
Questioning the right and the left
Unbalanced, off centered, off track
From our chosen path
Distorted Peace
    Inner Greed
    Societal Greed
    World Greed
Imperfect Peace
Singular focus on inner turmoil
Singular focus on societal demise
Collective focus on upsetting
The balance of man
Bringing forth hate and disdain for life
Distorted Peace
    Inner Greed
    Societal Greed
    World Greed
Imperfect Peace
The world is no longer our oyster
The mountain we wanted to climb
Is a sheer illusion
Dreams become tinged
Our palette bears the nasty colors of hate
Peace, in any form becomes unobtainable
Peace
    Inner Peace
    Societal Peace
    World Peace
Perfect peace still obtainable

Reflect, for full circle we come
As round as the sun, moon, and earth
We come back to self
Asking what went wrong
How did I contribute to cynicism?
How did I contribute to crime, hatred, and disdain?
Look to self
The reality is that we reap what we sow
For perfect peace comes from inner peace
Inner peace brings forth societal peace
Societal peace transcends into world peace
Peace
    Inner Peace
    Societal Peace
    World Peace
Perfect Peace

Quiet Reflections

In our quiet times, we dissect ourselves
Our inner person always speaking to us
The id, the ego, and the spirit
The message
Seek opportunities to improve, change, and enhance ourselves
Constantly question our motivations
Look within for our means to an end
Sometimes finding a haven that may manifest as a crime
A vengeance, retaliation
One that validates distortion
The clock ticks
Thoughts ramble and in our constant dialogue
Answers emerge
No amount of justification can erase the reality of the id, ego, and the
spirit
We see the speck of sand
We understand our single entity in this thing called life
We hear the calling from our spirits
We honor it by rising above conditions of our being
Unending, ongoing beats
That keeps us going on despite of
And because of our heart
Finding it, listening to the voice
Not altering the quality of my life based on negative circumstances

Dalliance with Life - A Life Lesson

We're conceived upon a notion of the greatness of our fate
With, and sometimes without, a forethought
We emerge from the womb, upon a clean slate
An undaunted idealism of our personal nobility
An openness to the thoughts and philosophies of the greats
That molded and shaped our destiny
One by one, we enter into the school of life
As individual as the moment of our conception
Not realizing the commonalities of our paths
We strike out to conquer the world
Taking the best from the best
The best from the worst
And sometimes, straddling the fence of indecision
Our clean slates soon become marred
However pure the intent, we embrace actions based on
Learned behaviors of our environment
Negative encounters which lead to self-defeating prophecies
Abusive prejudices that distort the soul
And send it spiraling to the depths of demise
Maybe, even vicious cycles of failure
The balance of our inherent nature becomes eroded
We become cynics of our grandiose dreams
We indulge in self destructive behaviors that illuminate our self-hate
We alienate ourselves from ourselves
Until there is no more discernment of us
We become drugged on the concept of nothingness
In our quiet times, we try to dissect our thoughts
To find out what went wrong
And question how we get back to the original safe haven of the womb
Sometimes, it is too late
The newly assumed haven becomes an excuse
An excuse to commit an offense against self
An excuse to validate retaliation
An excuse of be less than who we were meant to be
But, life goes on

We reflect, our thoughts ramble
And somehow, deep within, we find that which was once good
Our nightmare finally ends
We find our conscious
Our values become, once again clear
We remember that
We are a single entity in this thing called life
Life's spirit calls upon us to rise beyond ourselves
That we must feel the pulse
Of that which keeps us going on
Despite of ourselves
We regain our stride
We once again understand that our nature is good
We understand
That we have experienced and overcome our dalliance with life

Nature Framing Life

The forces of nature reach out to my being
A wonderful spirit surrounds me
My senses open wide as I receive the gifts it brings
Nature, calls of the wild
The glistening rain
The wind blowing through my hair
Brings unity of one
A sense of self
Energy that is as big as life itself
Nature, essence of my being
Becoming stronger, as I understand how I fit into the master plan
I become one with it
To fight against it is to face a destructive foe
To embrace it is to understand
My place in the universal scheme of things
For seasons understand
That winter calls for dormancy
That spring brings new life
That summer blazes in her glory
And that in the fall, we harvest the bounty

My Life, My Revelation

Oh, I've lived a life of anxiety, of pain, and of grief
I questioned, why me?
I asked, I sought peace, I looked for revelation
Seeking answers that only understanding God's love could provide
In my journey
What I finally realized is that to experience suffering is to be full-lived
To be sensitive is to be capable of telling the tale
To be intuitive is to be aware
To overcome is to endure and be strong
It's not been all bad
Don't fret and say you poor thing
For because of my experiences
I feel sunshine to the marrow of my bones
I feel the wind the same
I feel elation from the top of my head to the tip of my toes
I feel laughter to the innermost of my soul
I feel love to the epitome of the universe
I feel deep within
I hurt deep within
I live
Life has unfolded before me
Sometimes not aware of my path
Always embracing God's love and knowing that he'll never forsake me

I take the good
Blend it with unwavering faith
And emerge as a spirit-filled child of God
My life purpose has unfolded before me
I'm tasked with sharing my pain
Sharing my endurance
Sharing my triumphs
Sharing my faith
Even though sometimes unseen, even by me

The Eye and Ear of Discernment

Miracles never cease
Love for life is ongoing
A good seed brings forth seeds of eternity
We sometimes find a cocoon to passively lay in
Comfort permeates
Status quo seems the answer
Just a simple act of looking around
Hearing life
Provides evidence of the seed
Evident with a discerning eye and ear
An eye that sees the beauty of living
An ear that focuses on understanding the marvel of relationships
Family and friends
Present and nevermore
An eye that links to the heart
An ear that throbs, cries, and feels
An eye that can remove itself from misery and see the joys of life
An ear that knows of a better place
Beyond that which bitters the heart
An eye, an ear
Of discernment
Which we all want to use as a life focus

Stand Up My People

Stand up my people
For a triumphant meshing of souls
We are many, and yet we are one
Environments shape our future
But never our spirits
Toss the shield of preconceived rights
Shed the armor
That one's world is right
Stand up my people
To the count of eternal love
Follow the path that leads away
From vindictiveness, envy, and pride
Find solace in peace with self
Engage your brother to follow
Acknowledge and embrace
The factions who may share your heart
Honor individual convictions
Stand up my people
With humanity
Stand up my people
For one
For mankind.

One With Me, Two With Us

We have the need to be one with self
And the capacity to be one with another
Waking up, sharing dreams
Understanding that today is the day
To make those dreams become a reality
Understanding that on tomorrow, other sagas of life may unfold
With that mutual understanding
All aspects of our complement understand who we are together
Shared passions for life together
Shared sensitive sides
Tapping into each other's emotional being
One who knows how you like your favorite foods
One, that upon a kiss, all of your senses come alive
All pain subsides
One that together, deep bonds of intimacy are created
Bonds cannot be broken, only unleashed
Multi-dimensional aspects of life unfold
Making it, taking care of business
Doing what needs to be done for the unity of the two
Inherently living up to mutual aspirations
Understanding personal, unique, and unified driving forces
There is understanding of self
Waking up on a beautiful morning
Comfortable in your own skin
And capable of sharing self with the one you love

Venerations of Womanhood

Sense the pulse and full splendor of womanhood
Anointed of grace
Sometimes wearing entrapment like adornments
Hearts full of special places
Awaiting to be filled, re-filled, refined, or re-defined
Aligning with the woman within
Draped in the pureness of love
Draped like universal deities on our seemingly frail, yet strong bodies

Inherent to our spirit, we birth songs of pain
Strengths of nations yoke us
For we are the vessel of man
Never marred

Natures' marvels, embedded in our souls
Gentle and sometimes torrent
A bird's chirp
A spring rain
The crackling bolt of lightening
The thunder's roar
Knowing that in seasons, torrents will subside
Knowing that in seasons, peace in womanhood
Will reign forever as treasured adornments

Serenity and Dreams of Light

Pillars of light
Standing side by side
Blending with the light of the world
Creating blended lights within blended global existences
No boundaries - no parameters
Just light, two lights, blending into one
Side by side, amongst many lights

Subtleties of the wind, like their flickering paths
Sometimes causing a shift
Sometimes wreaking havoc
Always bringing peace when it subsides

Serenity that is as strong as the light
Serenity that is as strong as the collective glow
A single light standing strong for
Serene dreams of the perfection of two

Dreams of possibilities
Aloft as to where the lights shall shine
Where the wind blows
Another horizon, a safe place
The creation of other dimensions
Defined, refined, or re-defined

Serenity that is as strong as the light
Serenity that is as strong as the collective glow
A single light standing strong for
Serene dreams of the perfection of two

Some lights smolder
Engulfed by illusory beams
Trying to find the path to the true light
Of one, destined to be two

Serenity that is as strong as the light
Serenity that is as strong as the collective glow
A single light standing strong for
Serene dreams of the perfection of two

And when the foundations are truly shaped
Like rock and sand
Crystal clear become the dreams of man
The meshing of the lights are invoked

Serenity that is as strong as the light
Serenity that is as strong as the collective glow
A single light standing strong for
Serene dreams of the perfection of two

The Utopian Gift – In Synch

If I could
I would create Utopia
I would create synergy
I would create a world of peace
Dialogue would be in synch
Souls would be in synch
Love would be in synch
The world would be in synch
There would be no hidden agendas
Realities would be about embracing them
Life would be about living through it
Living would be about not losing ourselves in the process
If I could, I would grant a gift to each of you
It would be to live to the extent of your being
Be the best that you can
Impact society in your own positive way
Share your gift with the world
The reality is
I can't give you the Utopian gift
Only God
If only you reach out
Embrace his love and
Understand His messages of
Life, living, and love
Dialogue would be in synch
Souls would be in synch
Love would be in synch
The world would be in synch
The Utopian gift of being synched

Love Begets Love

Eternal feelings
Internal to the depth of external realities
From the source which nurtures
Love begets love

Eyeing, feeling, understanding
Being in the moment
The passion
The realities of that which can claim
The phrase coined love
Yes, Love still begets love

Is it defined in a bottle?
No, shatter that
Is it defined in a lifestyle?
No, break those bounds
Is it defined in a perception?
Open thy eye
For love truly begets love

No boundaries

Is it defined in a moment shared?

Is it defined in an hour of knowing?

Is it defined in a lifetime of existing together?

Yes.......love begets shared love in varying contours of life

Beckoning

If I beckon to you a sunrise
It means that I feel our serenity

If I beckon to you a sunset,
It means that I feel the comfort of
Our eternities together

If I beckon to you one star
It shall be the brightest at its most northern point

If I beckon to you my heart
It will always beam of hope

Beyond us, always perfecting our love
As us, always living our being together
Beckoning and answering the call of

Two souls

Always been destined to be one

Mornings, Mist, and Futures

On a beautiful morning
The veils are lifted
The rising sun glares
Through the trees
The crispness of the fall felt in the air
Commanding our attention
As the mist rises from the water
It creates its presence
Void of waves
Only peaceful waters and the mist
Sending a message
To the on-going flow of man
And in our man, woman, and child existence
A backdrop is created for our future
There is a gentle, sunlit rising to our approach to life
For the mist will rise of its own accord
And will evaporate as if it never existed
The sun will shine through its haze
Following a natural pattern
Of mornings, mist, and futures

My Personal Trinity — Me, Myself, and I

Self realization
Defined as a trinity of three
Me, Myself, and I
Me
Pre-destined
A singular entity
Fated to stand alone in the world
The palette designed
From the emergence of my mother's womb
The creation of my footprint
In today's society
I would be a benchmark
In the spiritual realm
I would be a path
In life
A soul destined to live as God defined
Myself
I earned my strength, my convictions, and my gifts
I melded with my world
At one with nature in my character building scenarios
Who am I to question?
Good, bad, and indifferent
Could haves, should haves
What ifs, why not, and I wonders
Spoiled, pampered
Catastrophes, finding my way
Making my way
Overcoming, becoming
I
Shifts and life lessons
The real "I" has emerged
No separation from the past
Total emergence
This person will never leave me
It is my evolution

Trinity truly defined
Full acceptance of who I am
Acknowledging my experiences
Heart not tainted
Bringing forth an acceptance
This is how we stay strong
This is how we stay focused
This is how we stay pure in heart
This is the melding of living
The trinity, me, myself, and I
Giving honor to a path
That was mine to take

Strength in the Walk

Strong enough to walk beside you
It is there, that we are balanced
Strong enough to follow you
For I honor your lead
Strong enough to bear your burdens
I am there to lend my shoulder
Strong enough to say carry me
For I may need to be cuddled for a mile

The Barren Tree

An outward appearance of starkness
Yet bound in an aura
A glow of love
Her barrenness is only a façade
For within her stark branches
There is the fruit of life
Branches, fertile enough to feed nations
Yet she saves the bounty for her nest
One seed sprouted
Surrounding her as an guardian angel
An angel of the original seed
A seed sown now in greener pastures
Awaiting her time to blossom
Seed of the seed
Seeds of their seeds
Seeds from which she shares her bounty
Strong, sturdy stock
Deep roots
For the seed continues to multiply
Even from her barren sap
Her limbs are still strong
For the guardian angel
Still shows her favor
For the barren tree

Life and Hope

Live, breathe, be
Milestones in life are just
Hurdles to overcome
Get through
Let go of the facades
Release the chains that bind
Life is to be personified in personal realities
There lies the ability to see beyond the quagmires
Dreams can be obtained
Shackles can be loosened
Paths forward are just a step away